DISASTERS
UP CLOSE

SPACE DISASTERS

MICHAEL
WOODS
AND
MARY B.
WOODS

LERNER PUBLICATIONS COMPANY
MINNEAPOLIS

To David Woods

Lerner Publications Company
A division of Lerner Publishing Group, Inc.
241 First Avenue North
Minneapolis, MN 55401 U.S.A.

Website address: www.lernerbooks.com

Library of Congress Cataloging-in-Publication Data

Woods, Michael, 1946–
      Space Disasters / by Michael Woods and Mary B. Woods.
         p.   cm. – (Disasters up close)
      Includes bibliographical references and index.
      ISBN-13: 978–0–8225–6775–2 (lib. bdg. : alk. paper)
      1. Astronautics—Accidents—Juvenile literature. I. Woods, Mary B. (Mary
Boyle), 1946 II. Title.
   TL867.W66135 2008
   363.12'42–dc22   2007030529

Manufactured in the United States of America
1 2 3 4 5 6 – DP – 13 12 11 10 09 08

Contents

Introduction

ON THE MORNING OF FEBRUARY 1, 2003, SEVEN ASTRONAUTS WERE RETURNING TO EARTH AFTER A LONG TRIP. THE MEN AND WOMEN HAD BEEN IN SPACE FOR SIXTEEN DAYS. THEY HAD TRAVELED 6.6 *MILLION* MILES (10.6 MILLION KILOMETERS) ON THE SPACE SHUTTLE *COLUMBIA*. THE ASTRONAUTS' FAMILIES WERE WAITING FOR *COLUMBIA* TO LAND AT THE JOHN F. KENNEDY SPACE CENTER IN FLORIDA. MILLIONS OF OTHER PEOPLE WERE WATCHING ON TELEVISION.

Columbia was flying at 12,500 miles (about 20,112 km) per hour. It was 39 miles (63 km) above Texas. As *Columbia* neared Earth, the air that surrounds our planet rubbed against the craft causing friction. As *Columbia* got closer and closer to Earth, the rubbing increased. It made the outside of the shuttle heat up. It glowed red hot, like charcoal in a barbecue grill.

Different kinds of insulation, or heat-proofing material, protect space shuttles. Some of the insulation is made of foam. Other insulation is made of heat-resistant tiles. Unknown to mission controllers and the shuttle crew, a small piece of insulating foam had broken off *Columbia*'s fuel tank during launch. The material had damaged the insulating tiles on the shuttle's left wing. As the shuttle heated up before landing, hot air poured into the left wing. Parts of the shuttle began to melt.

On the ground, mission controllers tracked the shuttle using radio signals and computers. They saw that one of the shuttle's tires had gone flat. About the same time, *Columbia* commander Rick Husband sent a radio message to mission control. But controllers could not hear Husband clearly.

Pieces of the space shuttle *Columbia* streak across the sky after the shuttle breaks apart over Texas on February 1, 2003.

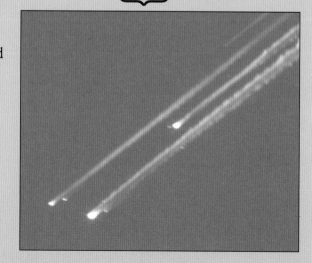

4

"*Columbia*," mission control replied, "we see your tire-pressure messages—we did not copy [understand] your last [message]."

U.S. Forest Service workers search for debris from the space shuttle *Columbia* in eastern Texas in April 2003.

"Roger," Husband responded. "Erm . . . . "

Those were the last words from *Columbia*'s astronauts. After that, mission control heard only radio noise and crackling sounds. The shuttle had begun to break apart.

People on the ground in Texas saw the disaster as it happened. Some reported seeing a ball of fire in the sky. Others saw the craft break into pieces. The pieces spiraled down to the ground.

All seven astronauts died in the disaster. *Columbia*, which had cost more than $1.2 billion to build, was completely destroyed. Andy Gallacher, a British reporter, was in Texas when *Columbia* fell to Earth. He described the scene afterward. "The school playing field is scattered with wreckage, from charred [burned] pieces of metal the size of a finger nail, to large chunks," he said. "The children of two farmers found the remains [body] of one crew member." With the loss of the expensive shuttle and the deaths of all seven crew members, the *Columbia* accident was one of the worst

What Are Space Disasters?

SPACE DISASTERS ARE SERIOUS ACCIDENTS INVOLVING SPACECRAFT. THE ACCIDENTS INCLUDE EXPLOSIONS AND FIRES. SOME SPACE DISASTERS HAVE HAPPENED IN SPACE. OTHERS HAVE OCCURRED DURING TAKEOFFS AND LANDINGS. SPACE DISASTERS HAVE KILLED MANY ASTRONAUTS. SPACE DISASTERS HAVE ALSO KILLED PEOPLE WORKING NEAR SPACECRAFT.

Unlike some other kinds of disasters, such as airplane crashes, space disasters usually kill only a few people at once. Only seven people died when *Columbia* broke apart in 2003. Yet the accident also destroyed an important and expensive spacecraft. *Columbia* was one of only four U.S. space shuttles. Building a replacement would have cost $3 billion.

After a space disaster, nations with space programs usually delay other spaceflights. Workers must check other spacecraft to make sure they are safe. After the *Columbia* disaster, the United States grounded (kept on the ground) the three other space shuttles. It took workers more than two years to make sure the three shuttles were safe. The repairs and delays cost billions of dollars.

All seven astronauts aboard *Columbia* died when the space shuttle broke apart in 2003.

6

"It sounded like a big boom. It rattled the windows for about 5 seconds and I didn't know what was going on."

—Adie Massaria, who heard Columbia break apart over Texas on February 1, 2003

Space shuttle *Columbia* takes off on its final mission on January 16, 2003, from the Kennedy Space Center in Florida.

HOW MANY DEATHS?

Nobody knows how many space disasters have happened. Years ago, the former Soviet Union (based in modern-day Russia) kept space disasters a secret. Soviet leaders thought that news of space disasters would embarrass their country. But we do know that from the time spaceflight began in the 1950s, space disasters have killed at least twenty-one astronauts. More than 150 workers on the ground have also died in space disasters. Other workers have been injured.

The number of deaths seems small compared to an airplane crash, which can kill hundreds of people at once. However, the death toll is actually quite large because very few people have flown in space. In fact, disasters have killed almost 5 percent of people who have ever flown in space. Imagine if accidents killed 5 percent of the people—one in every twenty—who ever rode in cars.

STAR SAILORS

In the United States and Europe, men and women who fly in space are called astronauts. The word comes from the Greek words *astron* (star) and *nautes* (sailor). Russians call their space travelers cosmonauts, meaning "universe sailors." The Chinese use the word *taikonaut*, which means "space sailor."

U.S. astronaut John Glenn *(right)* and Soviet cosmonaut Yuri Gagarin *(far right)* were among the first humans in space.

8

"[During a launch] you're really taking an explosion and you're trying to control it. You're trying to harness that energy in a way that will propel you into space. But there are a million things that can go wrong."

—astronaut Michael P. Anderson, who died in the 2003 Columbia disaster

MORE DISASTERS AHEAD?

In the United States, an agency called the National Aeronautics and Space Administration (NASA) oversees spaceflight and exploration. NASA works to make sure that spaceflights are safe.

But despite safety precautions, more space disasters will probably take place in the future. More and more countries are starting space programs and building spacecraft. Some private companies plan to take tourists into space. Someday thousands of people might fly into space on passenger flights. As the number of passengers and flights increases, so will the chances that disaster will strike.

MARS MONSTER?

When people count up space disasters, they include only accidents involving humans. But disaster can also strike unpiloted spacecraft (spacecraft that don't carry people). These spacecraft use cameras and scientific instruments to explore faraway planets and other parts of space. Space workers control the spacecraft from Earth with radio signals and computers.

Many unpiloted missions to Mars—the Red Planet—have ended in disaster. In fact, almost three out of every four spacecraft sent to the Red Planet have failed. Some of the spacecraft crashed. Others did not work properly. Some just *disappeared*. Space workers joke about the Great Galactic Ghoul—a Martian monster that eats spacecraft.

One of the monster's last meals was the *Beagle 2 (left)*. This unpiloted British spacecraft tried to land on Mars in 2003. However, the *Beagle* disappeared without a trace. The spacecraft stopped sending radio signals to Earth. No one knows its fate.

The John F. Kennedy Space Center in Cape Canaveral, Florida, is where NASA launches shuttles into space.

January 27, 1967
APOLLO 1

The command module of *Apollo 1* one day after a fire that killed three crew members

Three U.S. astronauts—Virgil Grissom, Roger Chaffee, and Edward White—prepared for a space mission in 1967. In their spacecraft, *Apollo 1*, they were supposed to orbit, or circle around, Earth. *Apollo 1* was part of NASA's Apollo program, a series of space missions leading up to an important goal: the landing of a man on the Moon.

On January 27, 1967, Grissom, Chaffee, and White were wearing space suits. They were strapped into their seats in *Apollo 1* at the Kennedy

Space Center in Florida. *Apollo* was on the launchpad. Its hatch, or door, was locked shut.

The craft was not getting ready to launch, however. The astronauts were just practicing. They were testing *Apollo 1* to make sure it would work properly in space. As they made the tests, they spoke by radio to NASA workers in the control center nearby.

At 6:31 P.M., Roger Chaffee radioed the control center: **"Fire! I smell fire,"** he cried. Four seconds later, Edward White gave more terrifying information: **"Fire in the cockpit."**

Workers in the control center watched *Apollo* on TV monitors. They could not believe their eyes. Flames burst from the craft. Workers began screaming, **"There's a fire in the spacecraft!"**

"Get [the astronauts] out of there!" yelled space worker Donald Babbitt. Suddenly, an explosion threw Babbitt up against a wall. More flames shot out of the spacecraft.

The workers grabbed fire extinguishers. Frantically, they tried to open *Apollo*'s hatch. It took them more than five minutes to reach the astronauts. By then the three men were dead. Chaffee was still strapped in his seat. Grissom and White had struggled to open the hatch. All three were badly burned.

Doctors later found that the men had died from breathing poisonous gases. The gases came from burning plastic inside the spacecraft. After the disaster, engineers used knowledge from the tragedy to make spacecraft safer.

"Fire! I smell fire."

—Apollo 1 astronaut Roger Chaffee

The crew of the *Apollo 1* spacecraft *(left to right)*, Virgil Grissom, Edward White, and Roger Chaffee, died when the command module caught fire during a training session in Florida.

What Causes Space Disasters?

WHY DO SPACE DISASTERS HAPPEN? THERE ARE SEVERAL REASONS. THE FIRST IS MECHANICAL ERROR—THE FAILURE OF PARTS OR EQUIPMENT ON THE SPACECRAFT. THE SECOND IS HUMAN ERROR, OR MISTAKES BY PEOPLE. FINALLY, "SPACE JUNK," INCLUDING OBJECTS LEFT OVER FROM PAST SPACE MISSIONS, CAN HIT A TRAVELING SPACECRAFT, WITH DISASTROUS RESULTS.

WHEN MACHINES FAIL

Spacecraft are complicated machines. A space shuttle, for instance, has more than 2.5 million parts. It has 230 miles (370 km) of electrical wiring inside. It has almost one thousand valves that open and close to let liquids and gases flow through. More than twenty-seven thousand pieces of insulation protect a space shuttle from heat. During a spaceflight, all the parts and pieces must work correctly. Valves must open and close at exactly the right time. Hatches must close tightly.

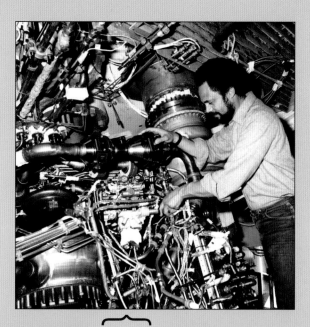

This technician performs maintenance on a space shuttle's main engine.

COLD TO HOT

Space shuttles must withstand very cold and very hot temperatures. In space, shuttles fly in temperatures as low as −250°F (−157°C). When landing back on Earth, shuttles get red hot—up to 3,000°F (1,649°C).

THE SPACE SHUTTLE:
HOW IT WORKS AND WHAT GOES WRONG

During the *Columbia* launch in 2003, a small piece of insulating foam broke off from the external fuel tank. The foam struck the orbiter's left wing, damaging some insulating tile. During reentry, hot gases leaked through the damaged tile into the left wing. The shuttle burned and blew apart.

The external fuel tank holds fuel for the shuttle's main engines. About 70 miles (113 km) above Earth, the shuttle jettisons, or releases, the tank. Most of it disintegrates in the atmosphere. The rest of it falls into the ocean.

The solid rocket boosters propel the shuttle into space. Approximately 28 miles (45 km) above Earth, the boosters separate from the rest of the shuttle. They descend by parachute into the ocean. NASA reuses the boosters.

The orbiter holds the shuttle's crew, cargo, living spaces, and work spaces.

During the *Challenger* launch in 1986, hot gases leaked from the right rocket booster. The gases burned a hole in the external fuel tank. The fuel tank exploded. The shuttle tore apart, and the orbiter smashed into the ocean.

If an important part of a spacecraft breaks, disaster can result. *Columbia* broke apart because some its insulation broke off. *Challenger* exploded in 1986 when hot gases leaked from its rockets. The gases made *Challenger*'s fuel tank explode. The explosion destroyed the space shuttle and killed its seven astronauts. On *Soyuz 11*, a Soviet spacecraft, three cosmonauts died when a valve failed in 1971. The valve opened at the wrong time. All the air escaped from the spacecraft. The cosmonauts couldn't breathe.

HUMAN ERRORS

People design and build spacecraft, and people can make mistakes. In 1996 scientists fed the wrong instructions into the computer on board *Ariane 5*, a European rocket. That error caused the rocket to tip over after takeoff. The rocket cracked and exploded.

Bad decisions are another kind of human error. For instance, officials at NASA decided to launch *Challenger* on a cold morning in 1986. Some NASA workers warned that the cold air could cause the shuttle's rockets to leak hot gases. But NASA launched the shuttle anyway. The rockets leaked, and *Challenger* exploded.

The weather was unusually cold in Florida on the day of the *Challenger* launch on January 28, 1986. Even the launch pad had icicles (below). The cold weather caused *Challenger*'s rockets to leak hot gases.

A flame can be seen near the external fuel tank as *Challenger* takes off in 1986. Seconds later, the shuttle exploded.

"We will never **forget them,** nor the last time we saw **them, this morning, as they** prepared for their journey **and waved goodbye and** slipped the surly bonds **of Earth** to touch the **face of God.**"

—U.S. president Ronald Reagan, quoting from a poem by John Gillespie Magee Jr. while honoring the Challenger astronauts who died during takeoff in 1986

SPACE JUNK

Space junk is another ingredient for disaster. Junk in space? You might think that space is empty. But it's not. Thousands of human-made objects orbit Earth in space.

Space junk includes hundreds of old artificial (human-made) satellites. Artificial satellites are spacecraft that hold electronic equipment. Some satellites pass along signals used for television, telephones, and the Internet. Others hold cameras that help scientists study and predict the weather. People started sending satellites into space in the 1950s. But when the satellites get old or break down, people don't bring them back to Earth. Instead, they leave the satellites in orbit.

A tracking device called radar allows space workers to locate old satellites. The workers can then make sure that spacecraft steer around the satellites. More dangerous, however, are smaller pieces of space junk. These objects include paint chips from old spacecraft and small pieces of metal from old satellites. Billions of these small pieces also orbit Earth.

TINY DANGERS

Even a bit of metal as small as a pencil eraser could cause a disaster. How? Space junk orbits Earth very fast. Some of it flies at 6 miles (10 km) per *second*. At that speed, a tiny bit of metal is like a bullet. It could crack a window. It could poke a hole in the craft. Then air would escape, and people inside the spacecraft might die. If a piece of metal punctured a fuel tank, the tank could explode. The explosion would blow the spacecraft to pieces.

So far, space junk hasn't caused a space disaster. But in 2006, the space shuttle *Atlantis* hit a meteoroid. Meteoroids are small pieces of rock that zoom through space. The meteoroid that hit *Atlantis* left a 0.1-inch (2.5-millimeter) hole in the spacecraft. Luckily, the hole did not cause serious damage to the shuttle.

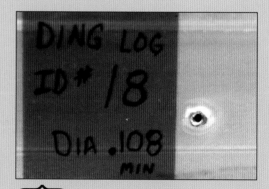

This hole on the space shuttle *Atlantis* is from a small meteoroid hitting the shuttle in space in 2006.

This satellite image from NASA shows all the space junk orbiting Earth. The pieces are much, much smaller than they appear in this image.

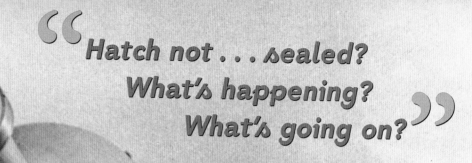

> "Hatch not . . . sealed?
> What's happening?
> What's going on?"
>
> —Soyuz 11 cosmonaut Vladislav Volkov

A Soviet *Soyuz* spacecraft ready to launch.

June 30, 1971
SOYUZ II

Everything seemed to be going wrong for *Soyuz 11*, a Soviet spacecraft. The problems began before the launch. One of the cosmonauts scheduled to fly the spacecraft got sick. Officials worried that he might have infected his crewmates. So a substitute crew took over. The new cosmonauts were Georgy Dobrovolsky, Vladislav Volkov, and Viktor Patsayev.

Soyuz carried the cosmonauts into space on June 6, 1971. In space, *Soyuz* docked (connected) with the Soviet Union's Salyut space station.

The cosmonauts climbed into the space station. They planned to stay for thirty days. However, the problems continued.

The cosmonauts planned to use a large telescope to study objects in space. But the cover on the telescope got stuck. The cosmonauts could not get it off. They could not do their study. Then a small fire broke out on the space station. After twenty-four days, Soviet space officials decided to bring the cosmonauts home early. The crew got back into their *Soyuz* spacecraft.

Before the craft disconnected from Salyut, however, a warning light flashed on. The *Soyuz* hatch had not closed properly. **"Hatch not . . . sealed?"** said Vladislav Volkov to mission control over the radio. **"What's happening? What's going on?"**

"Don't panic," mission control answered. **"Open the hatch, and move the wheel to the left to open. Close the hatch, and then move the wheel to the right six turns with full force."**

The instructions worked. The hatch closed properly. *Soyuz* disconnected from Salyut and headed back to Earth. As *Soyuz* commander Georgy Dobrovolsky prepared the craft for landing, he radioed mission control, **"Landing sequence proceeding excellent, all OK, crew is excellent."**

Seconds later, however, the crew heard a hissing sound. It sounded like air escaping from a tire. They thought the hatch had come unsealed. But the hatch was fine. The crew searched frantically for a leak. To hear better, they turned off their radios. Mission control waited to hear from the crew. But with the radios off, mission control heard only silence. Mission control thought that *Soyuz's* radios had broken.

Soyuz approached Earth normally. As it neared the ground, a parachute attached to the spacecraft opened. The

(Left to right) Cosmonauts Georgy Dobrovolsky, Vladislav Volkov, and Viktor Patsayev pose in the cabin of *Soyuz 11*.

parachute slowed the craft down. The space capsule made a gentle landing on June 30. When space workers arrived at the touchdown, they breathed a sigh of relief. The *Soyuz* looked perfectly normal.

When workers opened the hatch, however, they found that all three cosmonauts were dead. Something else had gone wrong on this jinxed mission. When the spacecraft reached 2.5 miles (4 km) above Earth, a valve was supposed to open to let in fresh air. However, the valve opened earlier, when the craft was still in space. When the valve opened, all the air rushed out of the spacecraft. The cosmonauts weren't wearing space suits, which would have given them backup air supplies. The three men suffocated (died from lack of air).

Danger Zones: Air and Space

A LAYER OF AIR SITS BETWEEN EARTH AND SPACE. THIS LAYER IS CALLED THE ATMOSPHERE. IT CONTAINS GASES SUCH AS OXYGEN. THE ATMOSPHERE IS THICKEST—CONTAINS THE MOST GASES— AT GROUND LEVEL. THE HIGHER YOU GO ABOVE THE GROUND, THE THINNER THE AIR BECOMES. EVENTUALLY, ABOUT 62 MILES (100 KM) ABOVE THE GROUND, THE AIR DISAPPEARS AND SPACE BEGINS.

Spacecraft are designed to take off from Earth, fly through the atmosphere, and then fly through space. Some spacecraft, such as space shuttles, are also designed to return to Earth, passing back through the atmosphere to land on the ground. Space disasters can happen during any part of this process: on the ground, in the atmosphere, or in space.

DISASTROUS UPS

Some of the worst space disasters have occurred during launch. During launch, a spacecraft must work at full power to reach space. As it zooms through the atmosphere, its mechanical parts are under great stress. If a mechanical problem occurs during launch, astronauts and space workers have little time to solve it. Before they find the problem and

SUPER SLURPER

During launch, a space shuttle's main engines slurp up fuel quickly. Imagine a backyard swimming pool filled with rocket fuel. During launch, the shuttle's engines would drain the pool in about twenty-five seconds.

fix it, the craft could come crashing down to the ground.

Rockets are engines that propel spacecraft into space. Workers load rockets with fuel during launch. A full load of rocket fuel makes a spacecraft very heavy. The rockets must work perfectly to lift all that weight. Even a small problem with the rockets can cause a crash during launch.

DANGEROUS DOWNS

The trip back home is another danger zone. Spacecraft reenter Earth's atmosphere at about 17,000 miles (27,000 km) per hour. At that speed, friction against the spacecraft heats it up. The sides of the spacecraft glow red hot. Temperatures reach nearly 3,000°F (1,649°C). Normally, insulation protects spacecraft from the heat. But if the insulation has cracks or holes, as *Columbia*'s did, the vehicle will burn up.

The space shuttle *Columbia* touches down in May 1998. The shuttle's parachute helps slow it down.

GROUND ZERO

Even on the ground, spacecraft are not safe from disasters. The *Apollo 1* astronauts died when fire broke out in their spacecraft during a practice session on the ground.

Space workers face danger on the ground too. For instance, in 1964 three workers were putting together a satellite inside a building in Cape Canaveral, Florida. The satellite's engine started by accident. Hot gases filled the room and burned the workers to death. In 2003 the nation of Brazil prepared to launch satellites into space. But a few days before the launch, the rocket for carrying the satellites exploded on the ground. The explosion killed twenty-one space workers and scientists.

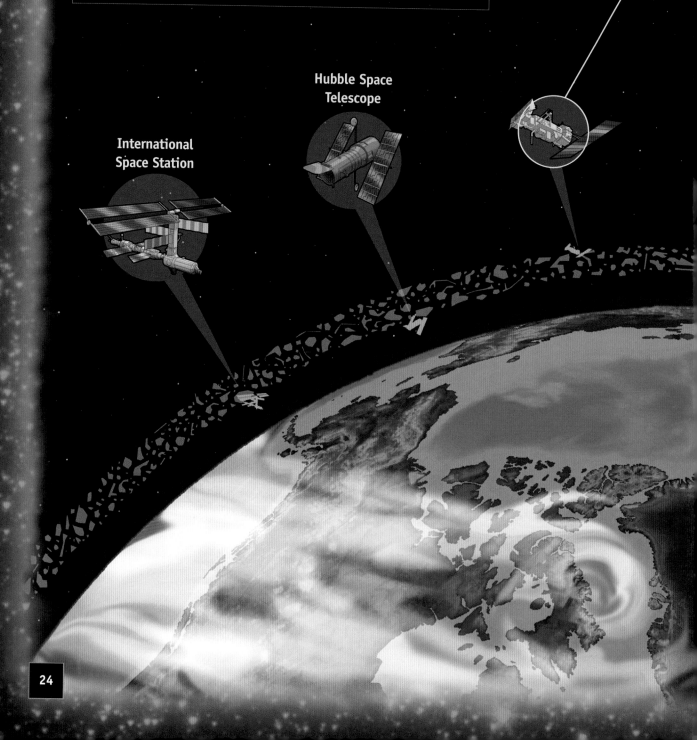

DANGER ZONES

Space disasters can happen anywhere spacecraft travel—on Earth, in orbit around Earth, near the International Space Station or Hubble Space Telescope, or near satellites, and even farther out in space.

Hubble Space
Telescope

International
Space Station

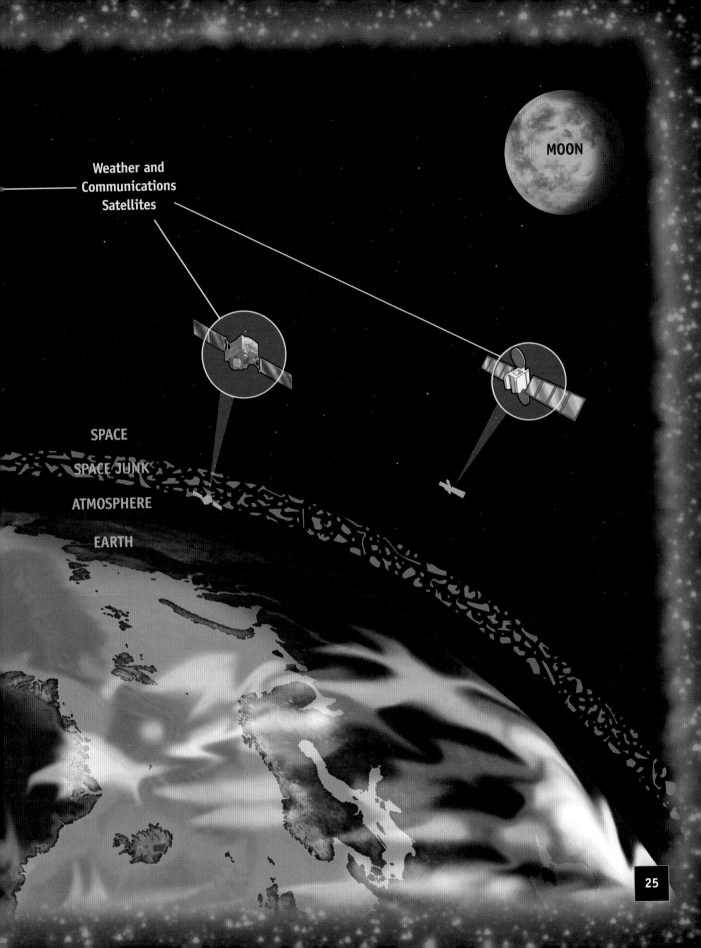

Weather and
Communications
Satellites

MOON

SPACE

SPACE JUNK

ATMOSPHERE

EARTH

25

January 28, 1986
CHALLENGER

January 28, 1986, was an unusual day for many American schoolchildren. On that day, millions of children got to watch TV in school. They gathered around TV sets to watch the launch of the space shuttle *Challenger*. Every shuttle launch is exciting. But this launch was special. One of *Challenger*'s seven astronauts was a schoolteacher. Her name was Christa McAuliffe. She was going to be the world's first teacher in space.

McAuliffe taught social studies at Concord High School in New Hampshire. All twelve hundred students from her school gathered in the auditorium to watch their teacher fly into space. McAuliffe's husband and two children watched the launch at the Kennedy Space Center in Florida. Her parents were there too.

Everyone cheered at 11:38 A.M. when *Challenger* rose into the air. At first, the launch seemed fine.

Challenger flew normally. The shuttle rose higher and higher into the bright blue sky.

About seventy-three seconds after launch, *Challenger* was 48,000 feet (14,630 m) above the ground. Then mission control got a radio message from *Challenger*. **"Uh-oh!"** said astronaut Michael Smith. That was the last message from *Challenger*.

People watching on TV and at the Kennedy Space Center could not believe their eyes. As they watched, *Challenger* exploded. Pieces of the spacecraft fell into the Atlantic Ocean.

Ryan Loskarn was watching the launch with his elementary schoolmates. **"I remember cheering, watching the split screen [TV] show of lift-off and Christa's class observing the launch,"** Loskarn said. **"Then I remember white smoke. A teacher screamed and students began to cry."**

"I'll never forget that day as long as I live," said Alisa Lipscomb. She was

Christa McAuliffe and other astronauts train in a zero-gravity aircraft for their shuttle mission in 1986.

a high school student in Conway, South Carolina, about forty-five minutes from the home of Challenger astronaut Ronald McNair. **"When I saw that explosion I felt like someone really close to me had just died right before my eyes,"** Lipscomb said. **"Ron was a hero to a lot of us."**

All seven astronauts died in the disaster. Some may have died during the explosion. The rest certainly died when the shuttle's crew compartment slammed into the Atlantic Ocean. It took recovery workers several weeks of searching the Atlantic to find the bodies.

Students at Framingham High School in Massachusetts watch as *Challenger* explodes after takeoff on January 28, 1986. Christa McAuliffe graduated from Framingham High School.

27

Measuring a Menace

WHEN DISASTER STRIKES IN SPACE,
PEOPLE ASK THE SAME QUESTIONS THEY
ASK ABOUT DISASTERS ON EARTH.
HOW SERIOUS WAS THE DISASTER?
HOW MANY PEOPLE WERE KILLED?
HOW MANY PEOPLE WERE HURT?

As with other disasters, measuring space disasters involves counting injuries and deaths. The *Challenger* disaster and the *Columbia* disaster each killed seven astronauts. The *Apollo 1* and the *Soyuz 11* disasters each killed three astronauts.

The loss of human life is always sad, especially for the friends and families of those who die. But when astronauts die, the whole nation (and often the whole world) mourns. That's because many people think of astronauts as heroes. They are smart and skillful scientists. When they travel in space, they put their lives on the line to help people learn more about the universe.

The crew of the 1986 space shuttle *Challenger*

AT LAST— ANOTHER TEACHER IN SPACE

In 2007 a teacher finally made it into space. The teacher, Barbara Morgan, had been Christa McAuliffe's backup in 1986. In other words, she would have flown on *Challenger* if McAuliffe had been unable to make the trip. After the *Challenger* accident, Morgan continued to teach school. In 1998 she switched careers and became an astronaut. Morgan flew into space in August 2007 aboard the space shuttle *Endeavour*. She worked as a mission specialist. She also conducted video question-and-answer sessions with students on the ground. The teacher-in-space program finally became a reality.

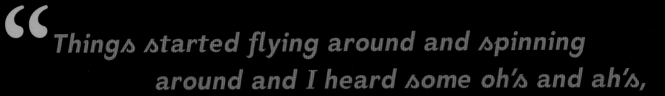

> *"Things started flying around and spinning around and I heard some oh's and ah's, and at that moment I knew something was wrong. I felt sick to my stomach."*
>
> —*Brian Ballard, Concord High School student, who watched the Challenger explosion from the Kennedy Space Center*

People watching on the ground and on television saw billowing white smoke as *Challenger* exploded in the sky in 1986.

ONE-OF-A-KIND DISASTERS

In addition to the human toll, space disasters also cause expensive damage. Space capsules cost hundreds of millions of dollars to build. Space shuttles cost *billions* of dollars.

Space shuttles are one-of-a-kind ships. The United States had only four space shuttles when *Challenger* exploded in 1986. NASA had a new shuttle built to replace it. That new shuttle, *Endeavour*, cost NASA more than $1.7 billion.

After disaster struck *Columbia*, NASA thought about building a replacement. But the cost was too high. By 2003 it would have cost $3 billion to build a new shuttle. The U.S. government didn't want to spend that much money. *Columbia* wasn't replaced. When space shuttle flights began again in 2005, astronauts had one less shuttle to fly. (*Discovery*, *Atlantis*, and *Endeavour* are the three remaining space shuttles.)

WHEN DISASTER ALMOST STRUCK

The *Apollo 13* spacecraft barely escaped disaster in 1970. *Apollo 13* was carrying three astronauts. They planned to land on the Moon. After traveling 199,990 miles (321,853 km), *Apollo 13* suffered an explosion. The explosion damaged part of the spacecraft, but the astronauts survived. The astronauts moved into an undamaged part of the craft, where they had air to breathe. They stayed there for the rest of their journey. They were not able to land on the Moon. Instead, *Apollo 13* looped around the Moon and returned to Earth. The astronauts landed safely.

Apollo 13 astronauts *(left to right)* Fred Haise Jr., James Lovell Jr., and John Swigert Jr. barely escaped with their lives.

NASA built the space shuttle *Endeavour* to replace *Challenger*. *Endeavour* has flown nineteen flights, starting in 1992.

DISASTROUS DELAYS

NASA uses space shuttles for different types of missions. For instance, in 1993 *Endeavour* went on a mission to repair the Hubble Space Telescope. The Hubble is a giant telescope that orbits Earth. Scientists use it to explore objects in faraway space. On other shuttle missions, astronauts have launched communications satellites, repaired satellites, and tested scientific equipment in space. When NASA grounds space shuttles, as it did after the *Challenger* and *Columbia* disasters, this important work stops.

One of the biggest jobs for space shuttle crews involves the International Space Station (ISS). The ISS is a large research lab that orbits Earth. It is also a living space. It has facilities for sleeping, cooking, washing, and other daily needs. Usually, the ISS is home to three or four astronauts. They live at the station for four or five months at a time. During their stay at the ISS, astronauts conduct a wide range of scientific experiments. The ISS is an international project. The United States and fourteen other countries run and staff it.

The space shuttle *Discovery* docked with the International Space Station in December 2006. The crews all shared a meal aboard the ISS.

The Hubble Space Telescope orbits Earth and sends back images of faraway objects to scientists. Space shuttle *Discovery* went on a repair mission to Hubble in 1993.

Construction began on the ISS in 1998 and is expected to take twelve years to complete. It is being built in stages. Space shuttles bring equipment and new parts from Earth to construct and expand the station. Astronauts wearing space suits are the construction workers. They fasten parts of the space station together during space walks. With each shuttle flight, the ISS gets larger.

Space shuttles deliver food, air, and other supplies for the astronauts living at the station. Astronauts who live at or visit the station also travel by space shuttle. Shuttles carry trash and other waste material from the ISS back to Earth.

The *Columbia* disaster grounded the U.S. space shuttle fleet for two and a half years. Without shuttle flights, the ISS could not run normally. Construction projects fell behind schedule. Russian spacecraft delivered a small crew and supplies to the space station. But the ISS could not operate as planned. Thus the *Columbia* disaster cost not only human life but also time, money, and scientific knowledge.

The space shuttle *Discovery* moves away from the ISS after completing nine days of work there in August 2005.

Astronaut Stephen Robinson is anchored to the ISS by a foot restraint in August 2005. He is repairing the underside of the space shuttle *Discovery* (not pictured). *Discovery* returned to Earth safely.

Two astronauts work on the ISS during a space walk in December 2006. Earth provides a colorful backdrop for their mission.

June 14, 1996
ARIANE 5

{ The *Ariane 5* rocket launches on June 4, 1996.

In Europe fourteen nations work together to launch spacecraft and study space. Their organization is called the European Space Agency (ESA). In the 1980s and 1990s, ESA scientists worked for ten years to build four special satellites. The satellites were supposed to study mysterious particles released by the Sun. These particles stream through space and hit Earth. They can affect weather and electrical systems on Earth. The four satellites cost $500 million to build.

On June 4, 1996, the satellites sat on top of *Ariane 5*, a brand-new rocket. The rocket was supposed to carry the four satellites into orbit around Earth. ESA had spent $7 billion to build *Ariane 5*. That project, too, took almost ten years.

After all that time and money, *Ariane* finally took off from the

The *Ariane 5* rocket exploded about thirty seconds after launching *(right)*. Burning fragments fell from the sky *(above right)*.

ESA spaceport in the territory of French Guiana in South America. The rocket was big and powerful. Observers could feel it rumble as it shot upward. Scientist Paul Murdin watched the launch. *"There were squeals, oohs, scattered applause and cheers as Ariane lifted off the launch pad,"* he said. *"The liftoff seemed so [normal]. Smoke and fumes trailed back to the ground as the rocket passed through [the clouds]."*

Disaster struck less than thirty seconds later. Scientists had made a mistake in the program (instructions) for *Ariane*'s onboard computer. Instead of steering *Ariane* straight up, the computer made *Ariane* tip to one side.

As *Ariane*'s heavy top tipped over, the craft bent like a drinking straw. The craft cracked, fuel spilled out of the crack, and the rocket exploded.

"We're going to lose this one," said an ESA worker as *Ariane* blew into pieces. *"A shower of . . . glowing fragments sprayed into the sky, trailing smoke and burning fuel,"* wrote Paul Murdin. *"All around me, most of the spectators fell silent. Two French rocket engineers swore . . . a woman sobbed."*

Scientists who had worked on the satellites for ten years were devastated. *"When it happened, there was a shell-shocked silence for at least two minutes,"* said scientist Nick Flowers, who watched the launch on TV from Great Britain. He added, *"We just sat there in silence. It is a loss for a generation of space scientists."*

Recovery

IN MOST DISASTERS, SUCH AS HURRICANES AND TORNADOES, RECOVERY MEANS HELPING VICTIMS GET THEIR LIVES BACK TO NORMAL. PEOPLE MAY HAVE NO ELECTRICITY AFTER A HURRICANE OR A TORNADO. THEY MAY HAVE NO CLEAN WATER TO DRINK OR NO SAFE PLACE TO LIVE. GOVERNMENT AGENCIES AND INTERNATIONAL AID GROUPS HELP VICTIMS REPAIR THEIR HOMES AND FIND NEW PLACES TO LIVE.

Space disasters are different. They don't directly affect large numbers of ordinary people. They usually don't damage homes and buildings. Instead, space disasters hurt a nation's space program. The country must ground other space vehicles until workers find and fix the problem that caused the disaster. Of course, recovery workers must clean up at the crash scene. But other workers have to study the crash, identify the problem that caused the crash, and get the space program back to normal.

PICKING UP THE PIECES

Recovery usually begins with picking up the pieces at the disaster scene. Recovery workers gather up the debris, or wreckage, for many reasons. First, the debris will give scientists clues as to what caused the disaster. Pieces of wreckage may have burn marks, for instance. Those marks may show that an explosion led to the crash. By studying the marks, scientists can learn why the explosion happened.

In addition, the wreckage at a crash site may contain dangerous materials. For instance, chemicals inside a spacecraft might be poisonous. Gases from the wrecked spacecraft might explode. It's important to clean up these materials so they don't hurt anyone on the ground.

Crews recover a piece of *Challenger* from the Atlantic Ocean.

The wreckage might also contain the remains of crew members. Crew members' families want their loved ones' bodies recovered. They want to bury the remains and hold funerals and memorial services.

RECOVERING *COLUMBIA*

A huge recovery effort began after the *Columbia* disaster in 2003. Debris from *Columbia* landed mainly in eastern Texas and western Louisiana. But some debris landed in New Mexico, California, Nevada, and Utah. Workers searched more than 2 million acres (809,400 hectares) to find wreckage and human remains.

Almost twenty-five thousand workers helped in the search. Some looked for wreckage from the windows of small airplanes and helicopters. Others searched on the ground. Divers searched lakes and ponds. It took about three and a half months to finish the job.

RECOVERY DELAYED

NASA grounded U.S. space shuttles for two and a half years after the *Columbia* disaster. The next shuttle to take off, *Discovery*, launched in 2005 *(right)*. Everyone at NASA was happy when *Discovery* launched. But disaster almost struck again. Despite all the investigation and study after the *Columbia* explosion, *Discovery* had the same problem. Foam insulation broke off and hit *Discovery* during launch. Luckily, there was no disaster this time. *Discovery* safely completed its mission. But because of the insulation problem, NASA grounded the shuttles again until 2006.

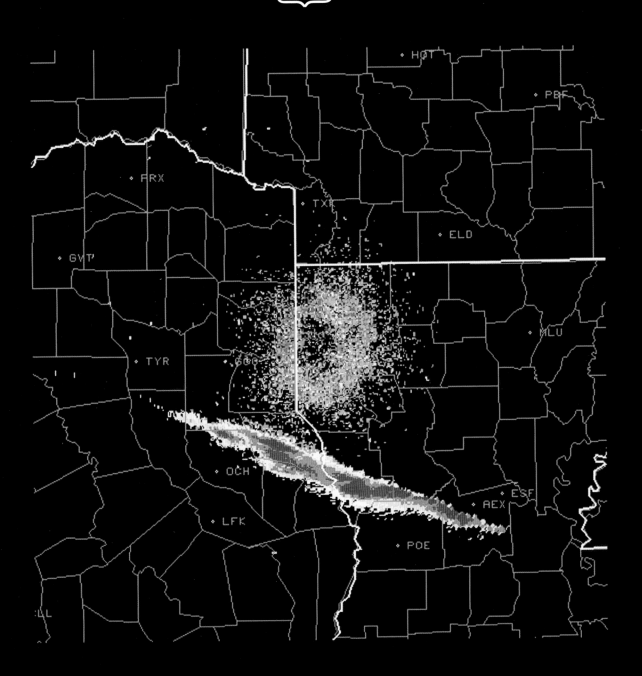

This radar image from the National Weather Service shows *Columbia* breaking up and spreading debris over Texas.

Many of the search workers were NASA employees. Others worked for state governments. Ordinary people also helped. For instance, some restaurant owners gave food and drinks to recovery workers. Some people told NASA about debris that had fallen in their backyards and on their streets.

The search for *Columbia*'s wreckage was sometimes dangerous. In wilderness areas, recovery crews had to avoid poisonous snakes and wild hogs. A helicopter crashed during the search. Two crew members died.

Workers recovered more than 82,500 pieces of wreckage—almost 40 percent of the spacecraft. Together, the pieces weighed 84,800 pounds (38,465 kilograms). Recovery workers also found the remains of all seven astronauts.

LIFESAVERS

People cannot normally live in space because space doesn't have any air. Without air to breathe, a person will die within minutes. Space also has no air pressure, which is the weight of air pressing down on Earth. Without air pressure, a person's body would expand like a balloon. It might even pop. A person in space would also face deadly temperatures and harmful radiation, a kind of energy. Micrometeoroids are tiny bits of rock and dust. They fly through space faster than bullets. A person in space would look like swiss cheese after being hit by micrometeoroids.

Spacecraft protect astronauts from these threats. Spacecraft have supplies of air for astronauts to breathe. Spacecraft protect astronauts from extreme heat, cold, and radiation. Space suits give astronauts the same protection. Astronauts wear space suits during takeoff and landing. They wear space suits when they work outside the ISS. Spacecraft and space suits must be sealed tightly so that air inside does not leak out. A leak can lead to tragedy, such as the *Soyuz 11* disaster in 1971.

> **"I'm devastated.
> It's unbelievable. It makes me so sad."**
>
> —Linda Steed, from Nacogdoches, Texas, a witness to the 2003 shuttle disaster

A big piece of *Columbia*'s engine landed in Louisiana in 2003. The 800-pound (363 kg) unit fell far to the east of most of the rest of the shuttle.

SPACE DETECTIVES

After recovering parts of *Columbia*, NASA workers put the pieces together inside a big building. The reconstruction project helped NASA find out what had caused the disaster. Workers also studied photographs taken during the launch and the explosion. They questioned eyewitnesses to the crash. The investigation took almost seven months. After *Challenger* exploded, more than 120 people investigated that disaster for four months.

Workers pieced together debris recovered from *Columbia* inside a hangar at the Kennedy Space Center in May 2003.

After both space shuttle disasters, scientists wrote reports about why and how the accidents had happened. They suggested ways to make spacecraft safer. For instance, *Columbia* investigators suggested ways to keep insulation from peeling off during launch. The *Columbia* investigators wrote a 250-page report. The *Challenger* report filled five thick books.

CHALLENGER MEMORIAL

A stone monument (*right*) to the seven *Challenger* astronauts is located in Arlington National Cemetery near Washington, D.C. The astronaut's faces and names are carved into a plaque on the stone. The monument also includes the words of a famous poem "High Flight." John Gillespie Magee Jr. wrote the poem in 1941. President Ronald Reagan included phrases from Magee's poem when he honored the *Challenger* astronauts in 1986.

When the VLS rocket exploded, it destroyed the launchpad too.

August 22, 2003
VLS ROCKET

The country of Brazil in South America dreamed of being a space power. It wanted to launch satellites into orbit around Earth. By 2003 only a few other countries—including the United States, China, Russia, and fourteen nations of Europe—had space

launch rockets carrying satellites into space. However, the rockets did not work properly. In August 2003, Brazil got ready to try again. A new rocket, called the VLS, was ready for launch. It would carry two satellites into space.

Three days before the launch, on

Some of Brazil's smartest rocket scientists were there. At about one thirty in the afternoon the fuel inside of one of the rocket's engines accidentally caught on fire. The whole rocket exploded in a huge fireball. The explosion was so powerful that people heard it 40 miles (64 km) away.

The explosion killed twenty-one workers, including some rocket scientists. It seriously injured about twenty others. The explosion also damaged the launchpad. It destroyed the rocket, which had cost $6.5 million to build.

Eyewitnesses described the scene. **"The launching pad collapsed and the technicians were working there,"** said Jose Veigas Filho, a Brazilian government official. **"We had just done two days of tests and everything went well, 100 percent,"** noted Brazilian air force colonel Romeo Brasileiro. **"Everybody is just devastated."**

Brazil had to hire and train new space scientists to replace those who had been killed. It had to build a new launchpad for its rockets. It took fourteen months before Brazil could finally launch a rocket into space. But the disaster gave Brazil's rockets a bad name. No other countries wanted to buy rockets from Brazil.

Before launch, Brazil's space scientists had high hopes for the VLS rocket.

The wreckage of the VLS rocket and launchpad, photographed three days after the explosion

The Future

Space disasters are terrible. They kill and injure people. They can destroy spacecraft that cost billions of dollars. However, space disasters also teach us lessons that can make spaceflight safer in the future. For instance, the *Soyuz 11* disaster showed scientists the importance of having astronauts and cosmonauts wear space suits during takeoff and landing. Engineers at NASA and other space agencies are constantly working to make spaceflight even safer.

THE CONSTELLATION PROGRAM

The United States uses its space shuttles to build the International Space Station. After that job is done, NASA will stop using the space shuttles. The shuttles may be put on display in museums, where people can climb inside them.

How will astronauts fly without space shuttles? How will they reach the space station to live and do experiments there? NASA plans to build a new group of spacecraft. These spacecraft will have new supercomputers that make them safer. They will be built with lighter, stronger materials. The new spacecraft will be part of NASA's Constellation program.

Constellation astronauts may fly to the Moon. (The last piloted flight to the Moon was in 1972.) They may even fly to Mars, where astronauts have never gone before.

COLUMBIA'S WORMS

All seven astronauts died on *Columbia* in 2003. But thousands of beings survived the disaster. Those survivors were tiny roundworms. Scientists had put the worms on the shuttle to study how the worms' bodies might change in space. The worms lived inside metal cans. The cans made it through the crash undamaged. Rescue workers found the cans while searching for the wreckage of *Columbia* in Texas.

Astronauts train in the newest version of the space suit in April 2007.

735 LBS

The *Orion* spacecraft—one of the new Constellation vehicles—will be ten times safer than the old space shuttles. For instance, if *Orion*'s main rocket explodes during launch, a small emergency rocket will blast the rest of *Orion* away from the explosion. Then a parachute will open. The parachute will slow *Orion* as it falls to the ground or water.

LESSON *NOT* LEARNED

Making spacecraft safe isn't easy. Many good ideas don't get put into action. That's because spacecraft are one-of-a-kind vehicles. They cost millions and even billions of dollars to construct. New safety systems are also expensive. They take a long time to build and test. Decision makers hesitate to spend the time and money on a new, unproven safety system—especially one that might never be used.

Workers unload a large section of debris from *Challenger* into a U.S. Coast Guard boat in January 1986.

The 1986 *Challenger* disaster offers an example of a safety lesson *not* learned. Recovery workers think that some of *Challenger*'s astronauts survived the space shuttle explosion. They may have been alive when their cabin fell into the Atlantic Ocean. If the cabin had had an ejection system, like that used on military airplanes, the surviving crew members could have escaped the shuttle. The system could have shot them out of the wreckage. They could have floated to Earth using parachutes. After the *Challenger* and *Columbia* disasters, safety experts suggested installing ejection systems on space shuttles. But equipping space shuttles with ejection systems would be costly and very complicated. Some experts doubted that the systems could be made to work effectively. So NASA decided not to install ejection systems on space shuttles.

NASA representatives show off
a model of the new *Orion*
spacecraft in August 2006.

DODGING THE JUNK

No matter how safe future spacecraft may be, dangers will remain. Space junk will be one of the most serious problems. As more and more countries launch spacecraft and satellites, more and more space junk will zoom around Earth like bullets. However, engineers are also building more powerful radar systems. The new systems may be able to spot even the tiniest pieces of space junk.

YOUR FUTURE IN SPACE?

In the future, you may fly in space. You and your family may be able to orbit Earth on a passenger spaceliner. Several companies have started taking reservations for space tours. The companies will take people into space on private (nongovernment) spacecraft. How much will a ticket cost? At least $200,000. A U.S. government agency, the Federal Aviation Administration, will make sure that private spacecraft are safe.

A few wealthy people have already become space tourists. They have paid Russia for a ride to the ISS and back in a spacecraft. The first space tourist was U.S. businessman Dennis Tito. He paid $20 million for a ride into space in 2001.

The first space tourist, American billionaire Dennis Tito, speaks with journalists from the International Space Station in 2001.

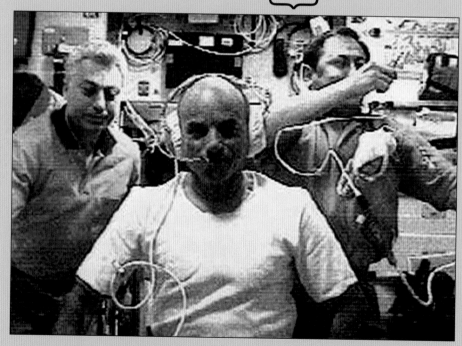

"The next time I go into space, I'll be able to take my family with me."

—Kathryn Thornton, former NASA astronaut, on space tourism, 2006

Space shuttle *Discovery* blasts off from Kennedy Space Center.

Timeline

1960 A rocket explodes at the Baikonur space center in Kazakhstan in the former Soviet Union. Ninety-one people die.

1961 Yuri Gagarin *(right)*, a Soviet cosmonaut, becomes the first human to orbit Earth. He travels in a spacecraft named *Vostok 1*.

1964 During construction of a satellite at Cape Canaveral, Florida, a rocket engine starts accidentally. Hot gases fill the room, killing three workers.

1967 During tests on the ground, fire breaks out in *Apollo 1*, killing three astronauts: *(left to right below)* Edward White, Virgil Grissom, and Roger Chaffee.

1969 *Apollo 11* astronaut Neil Armstrong is the first person to walk on the Moon.

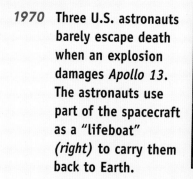

1970 Three U.S. astronauts barely escape death when an explosion damages *Apollo 13*. The astronauts use part of the spacecraft as a "lifeboat" *(right)* to carry them back to Earth.

1971 *Soyuz 11*, a Soviet space capsule, malfunctions upon landing. Air leaks out of the craft, killing three cosmonauts.

1980 A blast at the Plesetsk space center in the former Soviet Union kills fifty technicians. The Soviet government keeps the accident a secret until 1989.

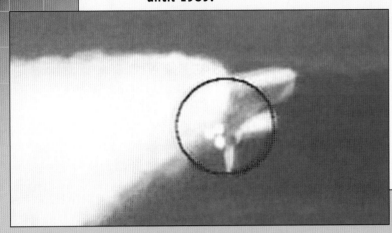

1986 The space shuttle *Challenger (left)* explodes seventy-four seconds after launch. The accident kills seven astronauts, including schoolteacher Christa McAuliffe.

1996 *Ariane 5*, a European rocket carrying four satellites, crashes immediately after launch.

1998 NASA and other agencies launch the first part of the International Space Station *(right)* into space.

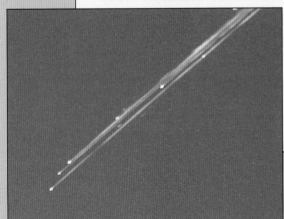

2000 Astronauts live in the International Space Station for the first time.

2003 The space shuttle *Columbia* explodes and breaks apart *(left)* as it returns to Earth. Seven astronauts die.

2005 Insulation breaks off *Discovery* during launch, but the shuttle completes its mission safely.

Glossary

artificial satellite: a human-made object that circles around Earth, the Moon, or another body in space

astronaut: a person who travels in space

atmosphere: a layer of gases surrounding a planet

cosmonaut: a Soviet or Russian astronaut

engineer: a person who designs equipment and vehicles, such as spacecraft

insulation: material that prevents the passage of heat, cold, sound, or electricity. Insulation on spacecraft protects astronauts and equipment from extreme heat and extreme cold.

International Space Station (ISS): a large satellite orbiting Earth. People can live and work at the station for months at a time.

meteoroids: small pieces of rock that travel through space

orbit: to circle around the Sun, Earth, or another body in space

radar: a device that uses radio waves to detect objects in the air and space

rockets: engines that propel satellites, space capsules, and space shuttles into space or through space

space: an airless region that begins about 62 miles (100 km) above Earth's surface and extends throughout the entire universe

valve: a mechanical device that starts, stops, or controls the flow of liquid, gas, or other material from one place to another

Places to Visit

Armstrong Air and Space Museum
  http://www.ohiohistory.org/places/armstrong/
  This museum in Wapakoneta, Ohio, is named for
  Neil Armstrong, the first person to walk on the
  Moon. Visitors to the museum can enjoy a multi-
  media presentation in the Astro-theater and learn
  all about the wonders of space.

Henry Crown Space Center, Museum of Science and
  Industry
  http://www.msichicago.org/
  The space center at the Museum of Science and
  Industry in Chicago, Illinois, offers displays on
  piloted and unpiloted space missions. Displays
  include the *Apollo 8* command module, the first
  piloted spacecraft to orbit the Moon.

John F. Kennedy Space Center
  http://www.nasa.gov/centers/kennedy/about/
  visit/index.html
  At the Kennedy Space Center in Florida, visitors
  can find out all about the U.S. space program,
  from its earliest days to future missions.

National Air and Space Museum
  http://www.nasm.si.edu/
  The museum, located in Washington, D.C., offers
  exhibits on the history of aviation and space
  exploration.

San Diego Air and Space Museum
  http://www.aerospacemuseum.org/visit/
  This museum in California includes exhibits on air
  and space travel, including the International
  Aerospace Hall of Fame. Visitors can even pilot
  the F-22 Raptor, a military fighter jet, in a
  simulator.

U.S. Space and Rocket Center
  http://www.spacecamp.com/museum/
  At this museum in Huntsville, Alabama, young
  people can attend Space Camp. There, they can
  wear space suits, eat space food, and even test
  out real space equipment.

Source Notes

5 BBC, "Columbia: The Last Communication," *BBC News*, February 2, 2003, http://news.bbc.co.uk/2/hi/americas/2717533.stm (August 12, 2006).

5 Ibid.

5 Andy Gallacher, "Nacogdoches in Trauma," *BBC News*, February 3, 2003, http://news.bbc.co.uk/1/hi/world/americas/2721929.stm (August 3, 2006).

7 Ibid.

9 Imaginova Corp., "Astronaut Biography: Michael Anderson, *Space.com*, June 30, 2005, http://www.space.com/missionlaunches/bio_mike_anderson.html (September 24, 2006).

13 NASA, "Disaster at Pad 34," *National Aeronautics and Space Administration*, September 15, 2006, http://www.hq.nasa.gov/office/pao/History/SP-4204/ch18-5.html (August 12, 2006).

13 Ibid.

13 Ibid.

13 Ibid.

13 NASA, "Tragedy and Recovery 1967," *NASA*, October 23, 2004, http://history.nasa.gov/Apollo204/chariot.html (August 12, 2006).

17 Ronald Reagan Foundation, "Address to the Nation on the Challenger Disaster," *Ronald Reagan Memorial Website*, 2006, http://www.reaganfoundation.org/reagan/speeches/challenger.asp (September 22, 2006).

20 Mark Wade, "Soyuz 11," *Astronautix.com*, 2006, http://www.astronautix.com/flights/soyuz11.htm (August 23, 2006).

21 Ibid.

21 Ibid.

21 Ibid.

26 Charles R. Grosvenor Jr., "Memories of the Challenger," *inthe80s.com*, 2006, http://www.inthe80s.com/dynamic/challenger15.shtml (September 17, 2006).

27 NASA, "Transcript of the Challenger Crew Comments from the Operational Recorder," *National Aeronautics and Space Administration*, February 3, 2003, http://www.hq.nasa.gov/office/pao/History/transcript.html (September 10, 2006).

27 Charles R. Grosvenor Jr., "Memories of the Challenger," *inthe80s.com*, 2006, http://www.inthe80s.com/dynamic/challenger11.shtml (September 17, 2006).

27 Charles R. Grosvenor Jr., "Memories of the Challenger," *inthe80s.com*, 2006, http://www.inthe80s.com/dynamic/challenger9.shtml (September 17, 2006).

29 William J. Broad, "The Shuttle Explodes: 6 in Crew and High-School Teacher Are Killed 74 Seconds After Liftoff," *New York Times*, January 28, 1986, 1.

37 Paul Murdin, "The Fiery Death of Ariane 5," *Journal of the British Astronomical Association* 106, no. 3 (1996):179–81.

37 Ibid.

37 Ibid.

37 Ibid.

37 Clive Cookson, "News: World Trade: Scientists Aghast as 10 Years Work Is Lost," *Financial Times* (London), June 5, 1996, 6.

37 Tom Wilkie, "Bang! Went $7 Bn Research, Pounds 500m in Kit, 10 Years Work, Dozens of Scientists' Careers and, Probably, Europe's Future in Space," *Independent* (London), June 5, 1996, 1.

43 Dave English, comp., "Great Aviation Quotes," *Skygod.com*, 2006, http://www.skygod.com/ quotes/space.html (September 24, 2006).

47 Jon Jeter, "At Least 21 Die in Rocket Blast at Brazil Base; Fire in Engine Causes Explosion during Pre-Launch Tests; 20 Hurt," *Washington Post*, August 23, 2003, A14.

47 *Taipei Times*, "Brazil Shocked at Rocket Deaths," August 24, 2003, http://www.taipeitimes.com/ News/world/archives/2003/08/24/2003065045 (September 16, 2006).

47 Jeter, "At Least 21 Die."

53 English, "Great Aviation Quotes."

Selected Bibliography

Cable News Network. "Lost: Space Shuttle Columbia." August 23, 2003. http://www.cnn.com/SPECIALS/2003/shuttle/8/23/2003 (August 28, 2006).

Challenger Center for Space Science Education. 2006. http://www.challenger.org (August 25, 2006).

Husband, Evelyn. *High Calling: The Courageous Life and Faith of Space Shuttle Columbia Commander Rick Husband.* Nashville: Thomas Nelson, 2003.

Imaginova Corporation. "Mission Columbia: Marathon Research in Space." 1999. http://www.space.com/shuttlemissions (July 2, 2006).

Lawrence, Richard Russell. *The Mammoth Book of Space Exploration and Disasters.* London: Robinson, 2005.

Lovell, James, and Jeffrey Kluger. *Lost Moon: The Perilous Voyage of Apollo 13.* New York: Houghton Mifflin, 1994.

Macidull, John C. *Challenger's Shadow: Did Government and Industry Management Kill Seven Astronauts?* Coral Springs, FL: Lumina Press, 2002.

Mullane, R. Mike. *Riding Rockets: The Outrageous Tales of a Space Shuttle Astronaut.* New York: Scribner, 2006.

National Aeronautics and Space Administration. "Experience NASA." NASA. August 25, 2006. http://www.nasa.gov/externalflash/nasa_gen/ (September 1, 2006).

———. "Space Shuttle Columbia and Her Crew." NASA. August 23, 2006. http://www.nasa.gov/columbia/home/index.html (August 27, 2006).

National Air and Space Museum. "Apollo to the Moon." NASA. N.d. http://www.nasm.si.edu/exhibitions/attm/attm.html (August 26, 2006).

PBS. "The Loss of the Shuttle Columbia." *News Hour with Jim Lehrer.* August 28, 2003. http://www.pbs.org/newshour/bb/science/columbia/ (August 27, 2006).

Reichhardt, Tony. *Space Shuttle: The First 20 Years.* New York: Dorling Kindersley, 2002.

Rense, Jeff, ed. "Space Disasters Since Exploration Began." *Rense.com.* 2003. http://www.rense.com/general34/did.htm (September 1, 2006).

Spignesi, Stephen J. *The 100 Greatest Disasters of All Time.* New York: Kensington, 2002.

Further Resources

BOOKS

Bortz, Fred. *Catastrophe! Great Engineering Failure-and Success.* New York: W. H. Freeman and Company, 1995. Bortz explains the *Challenger* disaster and five other engineering failures.

Briggs, Carole S. *Women in Space.* Minneapolis: Twenty-First Century Books, 1999. This book profiles women who have contributed in every way to the exploration of space.

Chrisp, Peter. *Space Station: Accident on MIR.* New York: Dorling Kindersley, 2000. This book explains a near-fatal accident on the Russian space station *Mir*, which nearly collided with a supply ship.

Cole, Michael D. *Apollo 13: Space Emergency.* Springfield, NJ: Enslow, 1995. This is the terrifying story of the accident on *Apollo 13*, which almost killed the crew.

Dyson, Marianne J. *Space Station Science: Life in Free Fall.* New York: Scholastic, 1999. The author, a former NASA mission control specialist, explains the workings of the International Space Station.

Fahey, Kathleen. Challenger *and* Columbia. Milwaukee: Gareth Stevens, 2005. This title for young readers examines both space shuttle disasters, which horrified the world and forced NASA to reexamine its safety systems.

Koppes, Steven. *Killer Rocks from Outer Space: Asteroids, Comets, and Meteors.* Minneapolis: Twenty-First Century Books, 2004. This book explores the impact of asteroids, comets, and meteors hitting Earth, from sixty-five million years ago, when the dinosaurs became extinct, to modern times.

Lieurance, Suzanne. *The Space Shuttle* Challenger *Disaster in American History.* Springfield, NJ: Enslow, 2001. This book emphasizes the historical impact of the *Challenger* tragedy. The book includes information about the astronauts who lost their lives.

Verger, Fernand. *The Cambridge Encyclopedia of Space: Missions, Applications, and Exploration.* New York: Cambridge University Press, 2003. This book is a valuable reference resource for people interested in how governments use space exploration.

Vogt, Gregory. *Disasters in Space Exploration.* Brookfield, CT: Millbrook, 2003. Vogt provides a clear explanation of the dangers involved in space exploration, with an interesting analysis of the *Columbia* accident of 2003.

Woodford, Chris. *Air and Space Travel.* New York: Facts on File, 2004. This book gives an overview of the history of flight, from very early attempts to the International Space Station.

WEBSITES AND FILMS

Blast Off: True Stories from the Final Frontier. VHS. New York: Discovery Channel, 1999.
Actor Ed Harris narrates this video, which provides an overview of the various people involved in a space project.

History of Space Exploration
http://www.solarviews.com/eng/history.htm
This website offers a wonderful collection of information about space programs in the United States and other countries, with photos and summaries of the missions.

IMAX: Space Station. DVD. Mississauga, ON: IMAX Corporation, 2002.
This movie takes you on a trip from the Kennedy Space Center in Florida to the International Space Station in orbit above Earth.

NASA: Fifty Years of Space Exploration. DVD. New York: Discovery Channel, 2003.
This five-DVD set examines the triumphs and tragedies of the U.S. space program.

NASA Kids Main Page
http://www.nasa.gov/audience/forkids/home/index.html
This site from NASA includes plenty of fun activities to teach you about space. You can even make a gingerbread rocket.

The Race to the Moon. DVD. New York: History Channel, 2004.
Join reporter Mike Wallace as he explains the early days of the space program, with all its successes and failures.

To the Moon and Back
http://www.fi.edu/pieces/hiley/
The Science Museum of London and the Franklin Institute of Philadelphia maintain this site, which contains information about *Apollo 8*, the first piloted trip to the Moon. Here you can also find an interactive quiz and neat jigsaw puzzles.

Women of NASA
http://quest.arc.nasa.gov/women/intro.html
At this website, visitors will learn all about women who have worked in the U.S. space program.

Index

Photo Acknowledgments

The images in this book are used with the permission of: NASA/HQ/GRIN, pp. 1, 12, 30, 54 (top); NASA/JPL-Caltech/GSFC, all page backgrounds; NASA/KSC, pp. 3, 5, 16, 23, 29, 39, 44 (top), 53; AP Photo/Jason Hutchinson, p. 4; AP Photo/NASA, p. 6; © NASA/ZUMA Press, p. 7; NASA/JSC, p. 8 (left), 13, 17, 18, 26, 28, 33, 43, 54 (middle and bottom), 55 (middle); AP Photo, p. 8 (right); © AFP/Getty Images, p. 9; AP Photo/Michael Probst, p. 10; AP Photo/Paul Kizzle, p. 11; NASA/SSC, p. 14; © Bill Hauser/Independent Picture Service, pp. 15 (both), 24–25; © NASA/Getty Images, pp. 19, 34 (bottom); © Bettmann/CORBIS, p. 20; © Hulton-Deutsch Collection/CORBIS, p. 21; © Mark Wilson/Getty Images, p. 22; © Keith Myers/CORBIS, p. 27 (top); AP Photo/Middlesex News, Paul Kapteyn, p. 27 (bottom); NASA, pp. 31, 35, 40, 49; © NASA TV/EPA/CORBIS, p. 32; © NASA/Action Press/ZUMA Press, p. 34 (top); © Alain Nogues/CORBIS SYGMA, p. 36; AP Photo/APTV, p. 37 (both); © National Weather Service/Getty Images, p. 41; © Karen Bleier/AFP/Getty Images, p. 44 (bottom); © Reuters/CORBIS, pp. 46, 47 (top); AP Photo/Alexandre Meneghini, p. 47 (bottom); AP Photo/Joe Skipper, p. 50; AP Photo/Pablo Martinez Monsivais, p. 51; AP Photo/Russian Space Agency, p. 52; © NASA-TV/Getty Images, p. 55 (top); AP Photo/Dr. Scott Lieberman, p. 55 (bottom).

Front Cover: NASA/JSC (main); NASA/JPL-Caltech/GSFC (background).
Back Cover: NASA/JPL-Caltech/GSFC.

About the Authors

Michael Woods is a science and medical journalist in Washington, D.C., who has won many national writing awards. Mary B. Woods is a school librarian. Their past books include the eight-volume Ancient Technology series. The Woodses have four children. When not writing, reading, or enjoying their grandchildren, the Woodses travel to gather material for future books.